THE DIVINE KILLER

To Mr John Campbell
with best wishes

Bunty Fraser

Photograph by Robin Grey

The author after his retirement

THE DIVINE KILLER

Roddie Fraser

GLEN
BOOKS

First published in 1998 by Glen Books
Shellcroft, Munlochy, Black Isle, Ross-shire

British Library Cataloguing-in-Publication Data

A Catalogue record for this book is available from
the British Library

ISBN 0 9528926 1 8

Cover:design by Artysans Inverness
Typesetting: Eric Mitchell, Glasgow

Printed in Great Britain by Redwood Books

The Author's family express their thanks to
Glen Books of Inverness and to Margaret MacRae
for her information technology skills.

Roddie Fraser BEM was an octogenarian, living quietly with Bunty, his wife of more than 40 years, on a croft overlooking Munlochy Bay on the Black Isle.

He was a distinguished detective, respected hotel owner and the Good Shepherd to some 40 sheep, each of which he seemed to know personally.

This is a little book about his life and is dedicated to Bunty, their four adult children and ten grandchildren, all of whom he loved dearly.

Sadly, just a dozen days after he finished this story of his life, he collapsed and died at his croft while working on the soil that was part of him.

His coffin was carried to its final resting place by uniformed officers of the Northern Constabulary, the old force he served for so long with distinction.

THE DIVINE KILLER

*The pursuit of the A9 murderer
by a Highland Detective*

I

Looking back over the years I have come to realise that I must have been born with the soil in my soul. I came into the world on the Black Isle, not far from where I live, on the 23rd hour of the 23rd day of November 1911, at a wee bit of a place called Upper Knockbain, one of a family of eight boys and one girl. My father was Peter Fraser and my mother Helen, and we grew up in a croft house, living on what my father earned as a road mending contractor for Ross and Cromarty County Council for whom he hauled the materials needed to keep the roads from falling to pieces. Part of his job was to maintain sections of the single track roads and to do this he travelled over long distances, using two Clydesdale horses to pull carts.

At Knockbain school I was a relatively quick learner and the two teachers we had there spent their working days preparing us for the high school. But I had just turned 14 when my father died and I had to leave school that day because there was no one else to help my sister and hired man to keep the road mending business. But the day came when the horse was overtaken by the lorry and we were out of business. Some of my older brothers were in the motor and haulage trade and I thought about going in with them.

The land and crofting seemed to be my only salvation, but stirring within me were stories of my mother's father, a man I never met. He was a policeman at Dingwall and his name was Charles Scott. I had heard much about him and how he died not only tragically, but very young. He had gone to help an ambulance man with a foreign seaman who was suffering from what was then known as the Black Plague, but what today we would call cholera, and sadly he contracted the disease and died very quickly. He was only 28 and his grave was sealed on the day of his funeral and has remained so to this day. It was not even opened years later when my grandmother died. These were hard times and he left behind him a widow and six children. She did have a police pension.... a penny a day every week for each child.

The urge to join the police became reality when two of my brothers, Alexander (later inspector with the old Inverness Burgh force) and William (to become a detective sergeant at the Flying Squad Scotland Yard) left to become constables. Once my mind was made up I realised the bit of education I had would never get me through the police entrance exam. So, at the age of 23, I went back to school, cycling seven miles each way five nights a week to get to Avoch School where I managed to learn enough to sit and pass the police exam. I was a proud man when my night teacher, the headmaster Robert Strachan, gave me a written testimonial which said I had 'fortitude of mind and a moral character of which I cannot speak too highly.'

And so it was, on May 29, 1936, I was sworn in as a probationary constable of the Inverness-shire Constabulary. The first three months of what was to turn out to be thirty years, I spent at our headquarters in Inverness Castle and then it was out into the world on my own. All the way south and westwards to the Kinlochmore beat, a one-man operation based at Onich. I travelled the 70 miles to get there by public bus, but when I realised just how large an area I was to police, I had to spend the then crippling sum of five guineas and buy myself some transport. A bike.... which allowed me to claim a monthly allowance of one shilling and six pence (now seven and a half pence) to keep it serviceable. I also got a free uniform and the use of a telephone. On top of that I was earning £2-12-6d a week and paying 25/- for my lodgings. I was left with the princely sum to squander, save or spend wisely of £1-7-6d a week or £1.37 pence in today's cash. While there, I made many good and lasting friendships. My landlady was Mrs MacInnes, a widow who had spent most of her life in Glasgow with her late husband, who was a native of Ballachulish. She was a most kind person.

The Author as a young constable

Across the road from my lodgings was the Post Office. The Post Mistress was one Flora Cameron, who lived with her bachelor brother. He ran a croft and did fishing in Loch Linnhe. Flora was a fluent Gaelic speaker, which for me was a God given asset as I spent many hours with her being taught how to pronounce the various name places 'Camus na Heiridhe', 'Camus na Gaul', etc. She also thought I should learn some Gaelic phrases for my sojourn in the West Highlands and possibly the Hebrides. One such phrase I always remember. It was 'Mach a seo' which she said I would no doubt find most useful on some occasions. I asked her what it meant and she said it meant 'Get the Hell out of it' if expressed in the proper tone! Another saying she told me I should never forget if travelling in the Hebrides was 'The Mull man will beat the Skye man and the Skye man will beat the Devil!'.

On my visits to Kinlochleven, at least twice a week while stationed at Onich, I always called on Sgt. John Glenday who, with his wife and family, resided in the Police Station at the Argyll side of the village. They were fine kind people. Sgt. John was one of the first two police officers who some time previously became involved in Police Federation matters in Argyll. This was frowned on by the local authority and resulted in the man, a Constable Morrison, being dismissed from the service and John being «exiled» to Kinlochleven with no hope of further promotion. John wasted no time in introducing me to the virtues of Police Federation activities which he emphasised was in the best interests of not only police officers and their families but also the service generally. Sgt. Glenday had with him there a

Constable Neil John MacCallum, a couthy, witty individual.

When on such visits, I often got a lift back to Onich in a grocer's van with Mr Angus Cameron, who with his wife Kate ran the grocery stores at Onich. On one such occasion, I was waiting for my usual lift, accompanied by Constable Neil John. It was 'Guy Fawkes' night and rockets and squibs were being set off all around by children, some landing at Neil John's feet! He suspected Angus of selling these explosives from his van, which was illegal and when Angus drove up to give me my lift Neil John leaned through the driver's window and asked 'Are you listening to the fruits of your travail?' The Camerons at the stores were most hospitable people and many of my evenings at Onich were spent in their home, often helping their three school boy sons with their homework!

As I pedalled my way around these lonely roads I never dreamed that one day in the far distant future I would be one of six young policemen from Scotland who would join forces with an up-and-coming MP and future Prime Minister to help draft better pay and conditions for Britain's police officers. Lord Callaghan and I were on first name terms. He became parliamentary spokesman for the police and fought to improve our conditions from the floor of the House of Commons. He was, and remains, a fine man and firm friend.

Eventually I made it through my two probationary years, which included three months at the training school in Glasgow. In April 1937, not long before I was transferred to the Lochaber divisional head office at Fort William, I had to report an unusual accident, but not the follow up. One day I was told that a bull had been killed falling from a high rock on to the Ballachulish-Kinlochleven road. The animal was owned by the Department of Agriculture and was being looked after by Bill MacKenzie. Two nights later I was at a ceilidh in Onich village hall and one of the artistes was a local violinist, who was firm in his Roman Catholic beliefs. It was a Friday night and at the interval I was having a cup of tea with the fiddler who would never eat meat on a Friday. He asked the waitress 'What's in the sandwiches, Mary?' She told him it was perfectly all right for him to eat one, ' because it's only Bill's bull's balls...' Over the years, in fact until the day he died, that old fiddle player and myself had many a laugh over the sandwiches at the Onich ceilidh.

Fort William was to be the place where I was to spend many happy years and I was there only a matter of months when something happened that was to change my life and introduce me to a sport I came to love through being forced into it in the line of duty. It was Easter 1938 when word came to us that a London doctor had fallen on Ben Nevis and was badly injured. I set off, leading what could be described as a rescue party, wearing my police uniform and boots and we went up the hill. The doctor had been glissading when he went over a drop and fractured his skull. It took eight hours to find him and get him down and away to Belford Hospital where, sadly, he died. The doctor's relatives thanked me for trying to save his life and when they realised how ill equipped I had been on Britain's highest mountain they handed me his ice axe. From that day on I was to use it every time I went on the hill, either for pleasure or police work. I still have it today and it is one of my most treasured possessions.

That first mountain rescue was to lead to countless more because it became essential that any mountain rescue team had to have an accompanying police officer to prepare a report for the Procurator Fiscal or other bodies who might need it. In the early days we had no special equipment. We had waterproof trousers and a windcheater, and eventually crampons we had to tie round our boots. Many a time we were on Ben Nevis when it was fierce and black, the snow blinding as we tried to peer through it with only the light of a police torch. There was no radio link to anyone, and once you were on your way up that hill all form of communication ceased. It was a case of learning something every day, mainly how to survive. In time I was to be appointed leader of the first official mountain rescue team to be formed in the Highlands.

I remember once being told there was a dead man on the Ben who had been killed in a fall. I went up in the dark with another officer and instinct somehow told me where the victim might be. Sure enough, with only the torch to light my way, I climbed to where the man was lying. We got him down and away to the mortuary and later one of the young officers who was with me was heard to tell someone. 'That Fraser is a tiger of a man. Not only can he find them alive he can also find them dead and in the dark.'

Many years later, in 1957, when I was a Detective Sergeant, my friend Lachlan MacKinnon, now sadly dead, but then Gaelic master at Fort William Secondary School and myself were the first mountain rescue men to be decorated when, in the New Year's Honours, we

The Author receiving his British Empire Medal

were awarded the British Empire Medal. The citation referred to 'Meritorious and courageous work in mountain rescue operations on Ben Nevis over a long period of years.'

But as I grew older and after exactly 20 years of rescue on Ben Nevis I went out for one last time. It took two days and a night and ended on almost exactly the same date as the first so long ago, away back in 1938. We managed to find the body of a climber on the south face and an RAF mountain rescue team arrived to take over from us because we were exhausted. As we descended, heading for a hot meal and a bath and bed, a radio message was relayed to me to say that Bunty had gone into labour and afterwards our third child, daughter Marion was born. I decided that day my family had to come first. I now had three children and thought they might just like to have their father around as they grew up.

II

THE WAR YEARS WERE HARD FOR EVERYONE, AND LIFE at Fort William was no exception. I was on duty never less than 16 hours a day, sleeping in the police office because someone had to be there to set off the air raid warning siren on the roof. We believed the bombers would come, targeting the aluminium factories in the town and at Kinlochleven. During one daylight raid, with the siren still sounding in the office, a German Heinkel bomber flew so low over the roof I instinctively ducked.

I worked away and in 1944 not only did things get better for us in the war, they got better for me, too. I was promoted to Detective Constable and the uniform was gone for good. Somehow I felt I was now a real policeman, although for years I had been doing CID work while still in uniform.

Three years later I got another move up, to Detective Sergeant, and my boss was a very fine officer based at Inverness, Detective Inspector Gregor Urquhart. Now he was a man of few words, but highly efficient. During the war, tinned food, blankets, linen and general things needed in case of emergency, had been stored throughout the Highlands in kirks, and this was the case at Rothiemurchus. But someone had broken in and stolen all the silver; so down I went with Gregor to start inquiries. He was a man who said nothing when he first arrived at the scene of a crime. For twenty minutes he would walk around, head down, head up, gazing into space, prodding and probing, thinking and looking, but never uttering as much as a cough.

As a young officer, many years before, I had come to know and like an old-time Highland sheriff, JP Grant, who always wore the kilt, even while sitting in judgement on his fellow man. He helped young officers survive the ordeal of giving evidence for the first time, always being sympathetic, and he was respected by us all. So it happened that day in 1947 I decided, while Gregor contemplated, that I would go along to the kirk graveyard where the old sheriff lay to pay my respects. As I stood at the graveside, fondly remembering the hours spent together, I noticed something behind the headstone. And there it was. A soldier's groundsheet and in it wrapped every bit of stolen silver. And to make it sublime, the soldier's name, rank and number were stamped on it. As Gregor walked around the kirk I called him to come over and see what the sheriff had done for us. Gregor is now 91 and every time I see him he mentions that fine day and asks, 'Have you been back to see the sheriff at all?'

I loved Fort William for many reasons. It was lucky for me, because I learned so many things there. I remember my first murder case as a detective in the town which was later reduced to culpable homicide. It involved a hit-and-run driver mounting a pavement and killing a man. I traced the car, charged the driver and decided we needed scientific evidence to convict, so I used a chemical to take hair and blood samples from the vehicle, then set off to Glasgow with it. And there waiting for me in his laboratory at the university, was probably the world's greatest living forensic scientist, Professor Glaister. That day I was to be given a crash course in forensic medicine that was to last me the rest of my service days. I couldn't believe it. There was I, a Highland bobby, being given a lesson, a sort of A to Z on what to do from the minute you started investigating a murder by the great man himself. I spent all day there and was soon to realise I was the only officer at Fort William who had such knowledge, and it dawned on me then that I was also the luckiest, because what I had picked up got me into many other cases that I might never have seen but for the professor.

Then there was the case of a well known local man who liked a dram and whom I arrested for drunk driving despite his claims that he was perfectly sober. He was bailed on condition that he would not drive until his trial, and the next week I accidentally met him at lunch. I sat beside him and it was obvious he had no idea who I was. The penny finally dropped for him when I walked into the witness box to give evidence at his trial.

I was still at Fort William when I was ordered on Royal Protection duty, to guard the Royal Family whenever they came under our jurisdiction in Scotland, whether it be on land or sea. Every year without fail they cruised through the Western Isles on Britannia heading for the Pentland Firth then Aberdeen en route to Balmoral for the summer. While they were at sea, I was aboard a fishery protection cruiser which was one of the escorts. Every time any of the Royals went ashore I went with them, accompanied by a soldier from the Queen's Guard. I remember Princess Margaret swimming at a remote beach on Benbecula. The Royal Family then had a picnic lunch while the soldier and I watched from a bit away. It was then that

Prince Charles and Princess Anne realised we had no lunch. Over they came to us with a picnic basket and shared it out. As we ate, the Prince, who was then just seven years old bombarded me with questions about the highlands and islands. I remember that he was particularly keen to learn the difference between a salmon and a sea trout.

I was already fifteen years in the police when I met Marion Bicket, known as Bunty, the girl I was to marry. Her widowed mother had taken her and her brother Leslie to Fort William to visit friends and they stayed in the boarding house where I lived. She was a physiotherapist in Glasgow, and a great part of our courting was a long distance affair. But I remember one weekend I was in Glasgow with Bunty and we went on the Saturday to the Barras, then to Queen Street to see my friend Donald MacLean from Skye who owned a big pub there. When we walked into the bar Donald took one look at Bunty and said to me 'Roddie, where in God's name did you get such a good looking girl?' I looked him straight in the eye and told him 'Donald, to tell you the truth I have just been to The Barras.' For years after that he would often ask me how my Barras girl was getting on.

During our courtship, I was sent in July 1953 on a six-month course to the Scottish Police College at Polkemmet in West Lothian. So every Wednesday afternoon and weekend, I was able to go to Glasgow to see Bunty. We got engaged on St Andrew's Night in Glasgow at the Sutherlandshire Gathering. It was a special night for us both, and for Bunty's mother,

Christine, who was a past president of the Sutherland Association.

But although romance was in the air, so was hard work. And at the end of the course I was delighted at my report. It said of me:

SCOTTISH POLICE COLLEGE

SENIOR DIVISION

REPORT ON STUDENT
COURSE A.5 (53)   CONFIDENTIAL

(13th July, 1953 – 18th December, 1953)

Name: Fraser Roderick   **Age**: 42 Years

Rank: D/Sergeant   **Force:** Inverness-shire,
                                              Constabulary

Police Service: 17.5 Years

Slightly under average police height. Wiry and compactly built.   Quiet with a cautious air of alert attentiveness. Modest and unassuming disposition coupled with a courteous manner. Played his full part in the recreational activities of the College. Keen on hill climbing and fishing.

This student showed that he has a quiet confidence in his own ability and a tenacity of purpose coupled with a friendly disposition. He gave the impression that he would be cool-headed, resourceful and sensible in his leadership of men with a good measure of firmness and decision.

He showed a good sense of balance, particularly in details, and reasoned shrewdly, precisely and logically when in discussion. He has the ability to express himself in an interesting and pleasant manner and holds the attention of his audience. He showed that he has a good sound knowledge of the practice and theory of criminal law and police work with a definite aptitude and interest for criminal investigation.

This student has made a good use of his time at the College and, by his own efforts; he has benefited considerably from his studies and his discussions with his colleagues. A keen student.

(Sgd) Ronald Graham
(Ronald Graham)
Commandant

Polkemmet House
18th December 1953.

Bunty and I married in 1954 and set up home in a police house in Fort William. Bunty never said anything, but I knew the only time she worried about me was when I went up the Ben. One of the happiest days in her life came four years later when I told her I was finished with mountain rescue work and would not go up again. And I never did.

Then, in 1959, I was promoted to Detective Inspector and made head of Inverness-shire CID and we flitted east to the Highland capital. It was a proud day for us both. In all our years together, I only remember seeing Bunty cry once, and it was after we had to leave Fort William for Inverness. I came into our new home in Inverness to find her looking out of the kitchen window at the rain, with tears in her eyes. She said there was nothing wrong with her, nothing had happened, no disaster. 'I'm just home sick for the rain of Fort William and the friends we have left behind,' she said. It's a strange old world when the rain makes you cry.

I found it hard to believe 23 years had passed since I had joined the force. So many years, so many memories. But I never realised that in three years I was to become involved with two murders, one of which was to make criminal history. I was eventually to come face to face with a psychopath; a gnome of a man whose name was Iain Simpson, whose sole object in life was a self-appointed mission to send sinners on their way to heaven. Not by repentance but with an antique .22 pistol. He was rightly to be called 'The Divine Killer'.

III

ON WEDNESDAY MARCH 7, 1962, I WAS IN INVERNESS ill with flu and unfit for work. As I lay there in bed that morning, some 400 miles to the south in Leeds, a man was getting into his wee car, and setting off for a ski-ing and hill walking Highland holiday. He was planning to spend a week around Aviemore, where there was heavy snow and the red deer were coming down from the hills because their shooting season was over and they were starving. No one knew that another shooting season was about to start. He was within hours of meeting someone as cruel and barbaric as the notorious Wolf of Badenoch, the half-brother of King Robert the III, who became feared throughout the Highlands for his murderous behaviour some two centuries earlier. And the tragedy of it all was that the man, George Green, need not have died. His murder was brought about by his kindness and forgiving heart.

The call that was to get me out of the house for the first time in a fortnight came on the morning of Friday March 18. It came from a retired police sergeant, Alexander Mathieson. He was 58 and working as a water bailiff. He was just south of Newtonmore after having checked his river beats and was walking back to his car, which was parked in a lay-by on the A9, the busy road that linked Inverness to the south. To get to the vehicle he had to cross the main railway line, then climb up a bank and get himself over a fence to reach the lay-by. There, stuck to the frozen earth, he saw a piece of paper and when he bent down and looked at it closely it appeared to be a bloodstained part of a map.

Carefully he picked it up, looked at it closely, then, with a policeman's training, put it back exactly where he had found it.

He then had a long look round and spotted loose branches and twigs piled in a hollow at the back of the lay-by. Then he saw a tourists guide book and beside it a rubber-covered torch. As he bent down once more for a closer look, he saw a shoe sticking up through the frozen earth, and in it part of a human foot.

It took the former policeman only a second to realise that he had stumbled on a hidden grave. Had he not come, what for him was an unusual route from the river bank, the makeshift grave could have lain undiscovered for many more days, even weeks, perhaps months. He quickly drove the three miles to Newtonmore where he found Constable John Stewart sitting at his desk. When he told him of the body and said it could only be murder, the constable rang his inspector at Kingussie. The hunt for the A9 killer had started.

I washed and dressed after the call informing me of the murder. The excitement seemed to have cleared my head and given me my strength back. At the Castle I saw the Depute Chief Constable, James MacIntyre, in charge because our Chief John Johnstone was seriously ill, and in fact dying. So off I went with my driver, Detective Constable John Cameron, and scene-of-crime officer, Detective Inspector James MacGeoch and Detective Constable Alan Forsyth, who was to handle all productions.

It was dusk when we got to the grave and nothing was touched until the photographs had been taken. We were slowly scraping away the earth from around the

The shallow grave concealing the body of George Green

victim's head when Dr. Henry Richmond, the Inverness pathologist arrived. He wanted to see the victim before carrying out a post mortem the next day. It was obviously the body of a man, fully clothed and lying face down. The only visible injury was a small bloodstained mark on his left forehead, about an inch from the centre and just above the left eye. Even at that early stage we felt it was a gunshot wound, probably caused by a small calibre bullet. We reckoned the dead man was 25–30 years old, just under six feet tall and weighing probably around 11 stone.

It was clear to us that his body had been well preserved by the cold weather but we had no idea how long he had been dead. But the only thing I did notice as we eased his body from the grave was how well dressed he was in green anorak, fawn sleeved pullover, white shirt, green tie and terylene trousers. On his feet were socks and brown leather shoes. It was obvious to me that he was not a tramp and I thought to myself that he might be a holidaymaker, perhaps a skier or hill walker. But he had nothing on him to substantiate that. He had no cheque book, letters, photographs or driving licence. All he had taken to the grave with him was 13/7d in cash and seven condoms.

By torchlight we examined his shoes and I told the others as we huddled round the body that our victim must have had a car because on the sole of his right shoe I spotted a worn circle, not more than an inch in diameter. And with that we had our first positive clue. I knew within myself that probably until the moment he was killed this man had been behind the wheel of a car. The wear and tear on the sole of that shoe could only have been caused by pressing it on an accelerator pedal. But where was his car? We came to the only conclusion possible. The person who killed the man in the grave had not only stolen everything from him but had also taken his car.

I left uniform officers to cordon off the area and stand guard over it all night. Then I headed back to Inverness. At midnight I briefed the Deputy Chief Constable, then examined more closely the articles we had found in the lay-by. Pencilled faintly on the back of the map that had triggered off the murder hunt, I spotted an address. No. 1 Lowell Street, Leeds. Could that, we wondered, be the home of the killer or the victim. It was 2am when I rang Leeds and asked them to go to the address first thing in the morning. Then I went home to bed. Strangely, the flu seemed to have gone!

IV

FOR ME IT WAS A RESTLESS NIGHT AND I WAS BACK at the Police headquarters in Inverness Castle by 7am. There were many things for which I had to wait. The victim's identity; how he was murdered; where did he live; how long had he been dead and, most important of all, where was his car? And in the back of my mind was one more thought. Whoever murdered this man must think his victim had not been found and he had escaped detection, and therefore I had to believe there was a high probability he would kill again.

The first of what were to be many disappointments came quickly. A call from Leeds police saying officers had been to number 1 Lowell Street and the occupants had no idea how their address came to be on the torn fragment of map or who the dead man might be. They thought they didn't know anyone fitting the description local police had given them. But also on the map was the stamp of a garage in the Yorkshire city; although the map might have been bought by a passing motorist I had the gut feeling either the killer or his victim came from the Leeds area.

I took time out from the office soon after 10am and went to the mortuary where Dr Richmond was about to begin his post mortem on the murdered man, and twenty hours after I had arrived at the lonely lay-by he phoned me and said, 'Your man was shot through the head and I have the bullet.' Now we knew for certain the cause of death.

The logistics of the inquiry were overwhelming. The A9 had to be searched along its verges near the lay-by and eventually for many miles on both the north and south sides. Officers with the description of the murdered man started to knock on every house door in Badenoch, and every garage was visited. But no one had seen the dead man. So we circulated his details to every British police force asking them if anyone could help identify him.

As I sat with the Deputy Chief Constable, we decided the investigation could well spread out over several parts, of not only the county, but Scotland and into England and we would need help, and that it was better to get assistance sooner than later. There was only one force that could send us men with the necessary knowledge and that was the City of Glasgow who had many officers highly trained and specialising in murder investigation. Mr James Robertson, their Chief Constable, was telephoned and asked for help and immediately promised to send his top officer, the head of CID, Detective Chief Superintendent Bob Kerr. He arrived that Saturday afternoon by car and when I met him at the lay-by, he had with him Detective Chief Inspector Jimmy Mclaren and Detective Sergeant Hugh Sloan. We had an on-the-spot conference and although I was out-ranked by two of the Glasgow officers it was agreed that I would be in charge of the murder inquiry.

One of the first things I told my own force officers was that there was no such thing as a perfect murder. However smart this killer thought he or she was there was always something overlooked and mistakes made. It was, I pointed out, our job to find these mistakes.

But the complications multiplied. The hills were busy with climbers and skiers and there was an extensive army manoeuvre going on in the region. It spread out over the Badenoch area, involved many men, some of whom had, by this time, left the district to return to their base in the south. I got other Scottish forces to interview every man who had been in our area and the army officer in charge remembered seeing a small dark car with two men in it at a roadblock. Later, much more was to come from this little fragment of information.

And sure enough our first break arrived. It came by telephone from Leeds police with help from number 1 Lowell Street. Although the couple at the house had not connected the dead man with anyone they knew, their daughter did. For several months she had been going out with a young man called George Green and they had even discussed getting engaged. But on March 7 he had left for Scotland in his car for a ski-ing holiday and she had not heard from him since. She had expected him back on March 14, and it was now the 21st. She knew of the A9 murder hunt for a killer, but never thought the victim could be the man she had planned to marry.

Before contacting the police she had been at a wedding reception and had told another guest her boyfriend, who worked in the same office as herself, had not come back from the Highlands and had failed to contact his boss. Coincidence is a funny thing and it was working that day in Leeds. As George Green's girlfriend was making up her mind to go to the police the following morning to report him missing, a bobby in the same city was looking at the details we had telexed about the murdered man and linking them to a piece of paper he was holding. It was a report from Mrs Marion Green of 28 Woodlea Street in Leeds, reporting that her son George had failed to return from a week's holiday in Scotland and had not been in touch with her. He had in fact now been missing for a week, she said.

Sergeant Barry Stevenson drove to Mrs Green's home to tell her that it was possible her son aged 30 might have been found. But, if it was him, then the news was tragic. Mrs Green told the sergeant that her son had left home early on the morning of March 7 for Inverness-shire on holiday from his job as an engineer with the Yorkshire Electricity Board. Then, Green's girlfriend, Sheila, was to tell the sergeant how she and George had met a year ago and played tennis together, but since she did not share his enthusiasm for ski-ing, she had decided not to go to Scotland with him. Selflessly, she explained that she wanted George to enjoy his ski-ing without having to worry about her on the nursery slopes.

Suddenly, after days with little information, I now had plenty, including the fact that Mrs Green told officers that when George left home he was driving his own car, a black 1957 Ford Anglia, registration number YUM 772. I told the murder team that the killer had made a major mistake in stealing the car because, as I correctly forecast 'It will lead us to him!' Logic dictated that the killer might still have the car in the mistaken belief that we had not yet discovered the identity of the victim. Within minutes I telexed every police force in Britain and asked them to make a special search for the car. I also gave details of the car to the press and asked them to make sure it got nation-wide coverage.

We still did not know the exact date of George Green's murder, but we now knew he was most certainly alive on March 7 and as his body was found nine days later it was probable he had been killed not long after leaving home and crossing the border. That was guesswork, later to be confirmed by his killer.

The car was our big lead because, although it was one of thousands, it had some interesting distinguishing marks. Mrs Green told us that both wing mirrors were broken, there was a GB plate on the rear, a special fixture had been welded below the boot for the spare wheel and the rear bumper was bent into the rear offside fender. We were looking for a mobile give-away.

On Monday, March 19, just three days after his body had been found, I met Mrs Green in Inverness and took her to the mortuary where she identified her son. She stood up well to the ordeal and was composed when she told how she began to worry when George not only failed to return home, but did not contact her. Then, almost as an afterthought, she gave me the second lead in the hunt for her son's killer. 'George was in the habit of picking up hitchhikers,' she said. An important part of the jigsaw had just fallen into place.

As we worked away, so did Dr Richmond. He rang me to say that a detailed examination of the victim's stomach revealed some undigested pieces of mushroom, suggesting he must have had a meal, probably an omelette, about three hours before he was shot. Out into the cold went the team once more, this time to check every hotel, restaurant and cafe along the A9 between Newtonmore and Aviemore, helped now by

George Green

eight Land Rovers loaned to us by the AA's Highland Patrol. The first result came almost immediately. At a Newtonmore restaurant, the waitresses remembered serving and talking with a man fitting George Green's description. Two hours later, we were contacted at the mobile incident caravan we had positioned in the lay-by where George Green's body had been found.

Eight miles south of where we sat, officers had found in the heather some bloodstained clothing and a holdall, which also had blood on it. It was lying in a stream nearby. The items in it appeared to match exactly what Mrs Green said her son had with him when he left home. The killer, confident he was far enough away from the murder spot, had dumped the clothing. We now also knew the direction he had headed with the stolen car. But what the man who shot George Green had failed to see was that the map had fallen from Green's body. The burial obviously took place in darkness, only three yards from the main road, and he did not notice that he had left part of a foot uncovered.

Reports of YUM 772 sightings poured in from all parts of the country, as far apart as London, Wales and Northern England. Each one was checked but we could not trace that little black car. YUM 772 seemed to have vanished! If it had not been hidden then there could, we unanimously agreed, be only one reason for its disappearance. The killer had changed the number plates!

I became intrigued with one report that came from an army officer whose men were now assisting us on the roadside search. He had not seen YUM 772 since we circulated it, but he had seen it BEFORE the murder was discovered.

It was seen on March 7, the day Green left home. He and his men were on manoeuvres near Dulnain Bridge and had set up a roadblock. The car that stuck in his mind had been stopped by the soldiers who remembered seeing two men in it. The driver was obviously wide-awake and talkative, but the man in the front passenger seat was slumped against his door, apparently asleep. The driver told the officer. 'He's had a bit too much to drink and he's sleeping it off...' They waved the car through, only to see it slide into snow and stick, it's wheels spinning. The soldiers walked from the roadblock, got behind the car and pushed it and the occupants back on to the road.

Somehow it seemed bizarre that the killer would have risked driving around with his victim sitting beside him. But the more I thought about it the more obvious it became. I reasoned that if George Green had been shot in broad daylight and if the killer was a stranger to the area he would not know where to hide the body. He could not risk leaving the dead man at the roadside because his body would be found almost immediately and police roadblocks would be set up throughout the country in minutes. So what else could he do but keep his victim in the car and hope that he might find a secret spot to bury him with the shovel Green always kept in the car in case he got caught in a snow drift.

I think I knew then that, without doubt, the army officer had seen the killer and his victim. And that he had spoken to the driver not long after the murder had taken place. The roadblock had been set up on March 7, the day Green drove north, so now I was positive he had been murdered the day he left home and had been dead for nine days when his body was found. The officer had a sharp mind and was able to give me a good description of the man who had been driving that day. It was most certainly not George Green. Then, some time later, I received a report from police at Fort William telling me that an English holidaymaker and his family had been driving on the A82 near Invergarry when they had seen the wanted car, its number plate still YUM 772, and two people were in the vehicle.

I found it almost impossible to believe, but it seemed that, without doubt, the killer had, about a fortnight after we found George Green's body, made some sort of macabre return journey to that area in his victim's car. Weeks later I was to discover that this was exactly what had happened and the killer had re-traced his steps. It seems improbable, but the killer must have driven once more past the lay-by where he had buried George Green. Our police caravan would have left that lay-by just a few days before.

V

DESPITE OUR NON-STOP EFFORTS, THE INQUIRY slowed and information trickled in. We ended the A9 search because I felt there was no chance of finding any more of George Green's property, which his killer may have discarded. We all felt strongly, however, that the killer probably kept some of his victim's possessions, but even the dead man's mother could not remember what might still be missing.

The elusive car continued to exercise my mind. Where was it? Dumped, or perhaps parked in a back street somewhere? Even more crushing, was the thought that it might still be in Scotland, even Inverness-shire. And although we knew the sort of gun used to kill Green, we still had no clue to its whereabouts. The chances of finding it were slim; the killer would almost certainly have ditched it.

We went back to the statements and re-read them. Had I missed something? I poured over them for hours, but still nothing jumped out at me. As I studied the statements, reports came in that the car we were so desperately trying to find, had been spotted all over the country. Every reported sighting was checked, thoroughly, but still we drew a blank.

Then from her North London home, Mrs Mary Hanratty, the mother of James Hanratty, due to hang in two weeks for the car murder of Michael Gregston, claimed in a newspaper, 'The A9 murder of George Green at Newtonmore has more than proved my son's innocence (he had been convicted of shooting Gregston and his girlfriend as they sat in his car at a lover's trysting place) and the A6 killer has struck again. Everything about this murder is the same as the A6. When I saw Jimmy at Bedford Prison he forecast the A6 killer would strike again. And he has!'

I had to admit that there were certain similarities. If the murders had been committed by the same man then Hanratty was indeed innocent because he had been in prison under the death sentence when George Green was shot. I could not ignore her claim so I detailed an officer to compare notes with the detectives in England who had investigated the A6 murder. In the end, I decided the two murders were not linked and the crimes had been committed by different men.

The jigsaw was slowly coming together, but there remained too many missing pieces for my liking. We built up a mental picture of the man we hunted. He was in all probability mentally unstable, with some form of criminal record, but not, we concluded, for murder. We asked all British forces to check mental hospitals for patients, out on perhaps a few days home visit, who had either failed to return or shown unusual behaviour when they did.

The car continued to haunt me. The question of its whereabouts flowed endlessly through my mind. Was it in England, across the Channel, in a loch or reservoir or hidden somewhere so remote it might stay there for years. I widened the hunt for it by alerting Interpol in Paris. I did not realise that this move would eventually produce the most unexpected result.

I had frequent meetings with the team involved in the murder hunt, because it was essential to keep everyone informed and make sure their spirits remained good, their minds active and their confidence high. I was to tell them often, that no matter the disappointments we would suffer, we had to keep going and that sooner or later we would get the break we deserved. 'Perfect crimes are for story books. We will catch the man who committed this murder.' But as I exhorted them to greater efforts, the Glasgow detectives had returned to their own force. I thanked them sincerely because I had needed them and they helped shoulder the heavy workload the inquiry put on our force.

But something crossed my mind as I re-read the statements. It was something the two waitresses at the Newtonmore cafe had said. Each time I read their words, I went back to what they said Green had told them as they talked while they served up his omelette. It was a weird story, about a hitchhiker he had picked up, perhaps around Pitlochry or Blair Atholl and I did not believe he had invented it. As he started to tell them he looked to the south out of the cafe window to the pavement where they all saw a small stocky man walk past, bundled against the freezing weather in hiking gear; anorak, thick roll-neck sweater, stocking cap and heavy boots. 'That,' said George Green to the two women, 'is the head case I picked up on the road.' The women described how the gnome-like figure resembled a bundle of wool on legs. So, alone in the cafe with Green, they sat down beside him as he ate, and listened intently to the bizarre story of the hitchhiking religious nut their customer had let into YUM 772.

Green told the waitresses how he and his passenger had exchanged pleasantries, until the little man had pulled down his sweater to show him a clerical collar.

What the hitchhiker was to tell Green left him speech-
less. His passenger told him that, when he was only
eight years old, he had been told by God to make a
light. So he went out and set fire to a haystack! As the
two women listened, Green told how at first he had
thought his passenger a religious fanatic and wondered
if he had been right to pick him up. Then he relaxed;
telling himself the man was not very well built and
therefore not a physical threat to him, and was in fact
harmless. Two hours later, that mistake was to cost him
his life.

Green told how the passenger boasted that, while still
a teenager, he had often read his bible from cover to
cover. By now Green told the waitresses, he was
convinced his hitchhiker was a religious crank. He
decided to concentrate on his driving and let the
stranger prattle on. The man who was soon to end
his life rambled on about how he had become an
encyclopaedia salesman so he could spread The Word
on his travels, but found there was so much cruelty and
meanness in the world that he decided to escape from it
all by committing suicide. He claimed he had then
tried to hang himself, but the suicide bid had failed
because God wanted him to stay alive.

As I read the words in the report, I could not help but
wonder why Green had allowed this strange man to
remain for so long in his car. Surely his alarm bells
must have been ringing!

In the cafe, the two women must have listened in
disbelief as Green went on to tell them how he became
increasingly concerned, but not frightened, as the little
man beside him revealed that after his suicide failure

44

people had started talking about him. Then he received another call, this time telling him he must enter an asylum and cast out devils from the patients. So as Green continued to head north, the man who was to murder him added, 'I volunteered to have myself committed!'

By now, he admitted to the waitresses, Green was having more than serious doubts about his hitchhiking companion. He explained the alarm bells finally turned to fear when his passenger told him he had simply walked out of the asylum after finishing the task God had set him. But then he had been arrested for stealing from a church and jailed for nine months. Green told the women how he had asked his companion then if he was in fact a fugitive and was slightly re-assured when he was told; ' I have served my time.'

Still struggling with his instincts which were telling him to stop and get rid of the hitchhiker, Green told the two women he had decided to change the subject and get away from religion. So he told the little man he was thinking about getting married. At this, claimed Green to the waitresses, the hitchhiker exploded shouting at him 'Don't you know you will be sinning'!? Then the hitchhiker proceeded to bombard his driver with biblical tracts all relating to sin and pornography.

At first, said Green, he was amused, and assured the religious fanatic that his fiancée was a fine Christian girl age 22 and old enough to know if she wanted to get married. But the passenger launched into another blistering tirade of way-out theology which at first amused Green, but then began to anger and upset him. He finally made his decision about the passenger. He pulled his car into a lay-by just a couple of miles south of Newtonmore and ordered his passenger to get out. The gnome-like man apologised for his behaviour, and despite the fact that he felt bad about putting him out of a warm vehicle into the biting cold, Green told the man that he had listened to enough of his drivel and abuse and wanted nothing more to do with him. His meal by now over and the little hitchhiker having vanished along the road north towards Kingussie, Green was to bid the women goodbye and added, 'I hope that guy gets a lift before I drive to Aviemore.'

As I read and re-read these statements about Green and his story of the little man he had picked up and eventually ordered out of the car I could not explain why but I suddenly had the feeling, and it was overpowering, that there was a definite connection between Green's murder and the hitchhiker. There was no doubt they had met then parted company. Green had told the waitresses he was glad to get rid of the strange little man, but life is fickle. Could it be, I wondered, that Green, a reasonable and caring human being, had changed his mind and stopped to once more pick up the gnome who got messages from God. If he had done so, then I had no doubt that this Christian gesture had almost certainly cost him his life.

The man I was so desperately hunting had, I was positive, never been in my hands before. But I concluded, that the elusive little hitchhiker had more than likely been in the hands of officers from another force and had most definitely heard a cell door slam behind him.

VI

I COULD ONLY GUESS AT THE SEQUENCE OF EVENTS after George Green left the restaurant. We knew that he had headed north on the way to Aviemore and that he could not have travelled far when, once more he saw the man who was almost immediately to kill him. Why he again picked him up no one will ever know. But the killer could only have believed that it was Divine Guidance that sent George to him for a second time.

I was later to learn from the man who pulled the trigger exactly what did in fact happen. Green stopped for him, leaned across from the driver's seat and opened the passenger door. He started to apologise for putting his passenger out earlier, and these were the last words he was to utter on this earth. Without saying a word, the hitchhiker calmly pulled an antique pistol from a pocket and, at point blank range, fired one bullet into George Green's head, killing him instantly. He then closed the passenger door, walked round the car and got into the driving seat where he pushed Green's body fully into the passenger seat shoving him up against the window and door jam. When he later detailed this to me, the killer was almost boasting about his efficiency. In a voice completely devoid of emotion, he took me step by step from the place he had murdered Green along the 70 miles of an unbelievable journey.

With a dead man for company, the killer calmly drove up the A9, through Aviemore towards Inverness looking, desperately, for somewhere to dump his victim. He knew there was a shovel in the boot, because during their first conversation together Green had told him that he kept one there for emergencies. The killer reckoned that this situation came under that particular category.

There were few cars on the road that snowy day as he eventually turned off at Carrbridge. In fact, for a long time, the only thing on the road was YUM 772. The murderer knew he had plenty of time, because Green had told him he was not expected back in Leeds for another week and it would be sometime after that before he was reported overdue. By that time, the killer was confident he could not be connected with Green's disappearance. He was also confident that once he had found a burial place, Green's body would never be found.

As the single track road weaved its way south, he turned a corner to find a lorry across the road, entirely blocking it, and there was nowhere he could reverse and go back the way he had come. Soldiers with rifles waved him down and he admitted that it was the only time he almost panicked. His relief was unbounded as he wound down his window to hear an officer say, 'Sorry to inconvenience you, sir. This is an exercise and we have set up a mock roadblock. Thanks for stopping.' Then he added, 'You are now free to proceed.' But the murderer, by now fully recovered, was determined to have the last word. Calmly, he told the officer of his passenger, who had not stirred during the minute the car was stopped, 'He's sleeping after having too much to drink at lunchtime. When he wakes up he'll think I'm joking when I tell him we stopped at an army road block.' But as he drove away the car slithered into a ditch and the soldiers returned to push him back on to the road, and off he went. Eventually, he got himself back onto the A9 and headed south towards the lay-by. He was to admit that by now he was more than a little anxious because, not only did he not know the area well, he could not, because of the snow, see any place to stop to dig Green's grave.

Then once more, he received Divine Guidance, 'Go back to the lay-by where Green put you out and hide him there,' was the message. He duly obliged, and as the lights of Newtonmore twinkled in the darkness, he pulled the shovel from the boot and started to dig and chop his way through the frozen earth. But in the darkness, he didn't see the map fall from the car nor, when he thought the body was fully hidden, did he notice part of a foot still sticking through the earth and twigs. His incredible journey had taken him two hours and he had covered this distance with a dead man sitting inches away from him. His heart, he was to tell me, was beating quickly and he was sighing with relief as he got back into, what he now considered to be his car, closed the door, switched the engine on and drove off into the darkness. Then nature intervened. It started to snow heavily and in a few minutes, the grave was covered completely.

Then, at last, perhaps due to luck, sleepless nights or the thoroughness with which the inquiry had been carried out, our information sent to every part of Britain, came the break I had forecast to the team so often. It was a piece of wonderful detective work, stranger than fiction, a case of intuition not by a policeman, but by a teenage youth who might well have been more interested in girls than cars. Fortunately for us he was not!

It started on the evening of May 4, exactly seven long and weary weeks to the day that I had gone for the first time to the lay-by to see George Green's grave. It might have been lucky, but that boy had the key that was going to unlock so many doors which had been closed to us, and provide the final pieces that made the complete jigsaw.

His name was Michael Davenport, just 19, and still learning about life. But he did know an awful lot about cars. He was in a peak hour traffic build up in Stockport Road, Manchester, on his way home from his father's garage and second-hand car business. Now despite his youth, cars had fascinated him literally from the moment he learned to walk. He knew within a second any car, the make and year it had come off the production line. As he sat there in a slow moving convoy of cars, he noticed a car that could not have been what it seemed.

It was instantly recognisable as a Ford Anglia but the registration number somehow didn't appear to tally with the car's likely year of manufacture. Of itself, that wasn't unusual but the discrepancy was sufficient for him to focus his mind on a notice that had been on the garage wall for almost a month now, relating back to a 1957 black Ford Anglia which the police were anxious to trace. He remembered the registration number was YUM 772. But the car he was following behind was two-tone grey and red and had a different licence plate. Yet everything seemed to fit the description given in the police appeal - both mirrors broken off, GB plate on the rear, special fixture for spare wheel fitted under the boot, rear bumper believed to be bent into the rear off-side mudguard. There could be no doubt that this was the car the police were looking for. The young apprentice mechanic was convinced that he had accidentally stumbled on the wanted vehicle.

Nearing Longsight police station, Davenport spotted a uniformed policeman getting out of a car. Winding down the window he beckoned to the officer, shouting, 'Don't ask questions, just jump in. We've got to follow that vehicle in front!' To the boy's relief, the officer responded immediately and, pointing to the car in front he explained to the officer, 'I think that's the car wanted in connection with the A9 murder in Scotland.' As the surveillance pursuit continued, Davenport had time to detail the reasons for his suspicions. Then they watched from a discreet distance as the car was driven to a lock-up where they saw the driver enter a house on Hathersage Road. 'Keep your eye on the house, until I phone for assistance,' the constable told Davenport.

Ten minutes later, police officers were climbing to an upstairs bedroom where they found a small, stocky man seated on the bed munching an apple. 'I suppose you want me for the A9 murder!' he said coolly.

It was six o'clock when the phone rang in my office. I had never lost the belief that I would eventually find Green's killer, but I admit there were times when I had to re-assure myself. My patience often wore thin, but I kept going, and more importantly, kept my murder team going. I often hammered home the message: 'We *will* find this killer!'

I was once more going over statements when I had to stop and lift the phone. On the other end was a man who identified himself as Detective Inspector Poole of Area Crime HQ at Longsight, Manchester. What he had to say that evening was the answer to all the baffling questions we had faced, and the solution to this unique murder. I will never forget his words. 'Mr Fraser, I think we have the man you are looking for.' And the next words he uttered almost took my breath from my body. 'The car he was driving was owned by Mr George Green. It now has false numberplates (yet another of our beliefs had turned out to be right) and the driver says he is a Scotsman, Iain Simpson, from Airdrie, Lanarkshire. He seems to have a fetish about religion,' (and the detective was telling me just what George Green had told the waitresses so many weeks before) and he claims he bought the car in a Glasgow garage.'

I felt the adrenaline rush through me as I listened to the policeman's report. Here, by telephone from 400 miles away, came the information I had so often told my officers we would surely one day get. I think I remained calm as I told that detective in Leeds, 'Keep him in custody and don't let anyone into his bedroom or touch the car until I can get down there.'

Then, with my driver, the reliable John Cameron, I left Inverness at 7.30pm that Friday night. I had rushed home, telephoning Bunty to tell her to pack whatever she felt I would need for a long stay from home and picked up the bag. I didn't even think of having a cup of tea. I had taken a minute to ring Detective Chief Inspector Jimmy McLaren in Glasgow and tell him what was happening and I told him I would stop off in Glasgow. In two cars we set off south from there. Never had a car trip of 400 miles excited me as much as this one did.

VII

A T 6.45AM ON SATURDAY, WE ARRIVED AT LONGSIGHT police station shattered. But a cup of tea and a bite of breakfast set me up for what was to be one of the most momentous days in my life. A local bobby took us to a lock up garage in Daisy Bank Road where Simpson garaged his car. One look at it convinced me that here, at long last, was the car I had been seeking for seven long weeks. The registration plate read DJA 20 and the road tax disc was numbered 0080083. It didn't take long to discover it had been stolen from a mechanical excavator at Aultbea in Wester Ross. But more significantly, the chassis and engine number was 100E 337869. And that confirmed it as the vehicle George Green owned. We had the car, now I was about to meet face to face with the man we had so desperately sought. I couldn't wait to see his face and talk to him. We had dreamed up a mental picture of him and his background. Was Highland foresight about to prove us right?

But before confronting Simpson, I went back to the garage to see the car. There were documents there which took me a moment to fit into the murder. Then I realised that they didn't fit at all. But they DID probably solve another riddle. The disappearance of a Swiss national, Hans Gimmi. His name registered with me immediately. I turned to the two Glasgow officers and told them, 'I know of this man. He was recently reported by Interpol to the Missing Persons Bureau.'

Exhausted, yet exultant, I now realised that I was about to interview the man who had almost certainly murdered George Green, and very probably had done the same to the man from Switzerland. I telexed Paris to confirm that Gimmi had not turned up, then went to the house where Simpson had been living. Hathersage Road was nothing special, but the contents of his room certainly was. We spent hours taking it apart, a little bit at a time, making sure nothing was missed. Everything was labelled, and it was clear that nearly all the items had belonged to either George Green or Hans Gimmi. Then I interviewed Simpson's friend Arthur Sale and now, without sleep for more than 36 hours, went at last to confront Iain Simpson, knowing I had enough evidence and forensic material to convict him of certainly one murder, and very likely two.

But I had to adhere to the letter of the law. I cautioned the suspect that distant Saturday night, telling him 'Iain Simpson, I am charging you with the murder of George William Green. You do not have to say anything, but anything you do say will be taken down and may be given in evidence.' I also charged him with stealing Green's car and his possessions. What, I wondered, would this strange little man, whose face I had so desperately wanted to see, say to that? The answer came immediately. He claimed that he had found the car in Upper Booth Street, Manchester, adding 'I knocked it. Last July when I was in Dumfries Infirmary I told Dr. Stirling that I was going to kill someone. When I was due for discharge from Barlinnie Prison I wrote to Dr. Stirling to ask if he would take me in as a patient. I heard nothing from him and I was discharged in January. But this was going through my head for a long time now.' As I wrote it down, there was a pause. Then Simpson, apparently quite untroubled and seemingly enjoying himself, added: 'I shot him! I'm glad I've been caught. I was going to do it again.'

Simpson seemed totally unconcerned, even relaxed as he told me slowly, and deliberately as I wrote it down, how he had murdered George Green. He had been offered a lift somewhere north of Pitlochry, and they had fallen out when he started to talk to Green about philosophy, the bible, social immorality, Frans Libido and things like that, he explained. Then he added, 'He ordered me out of the car just before Newtonmore then drove off. I came upon him again after walking two miles or so, maybe a bit more, and I had made up my mind before this that he was a menace and decided then to shoot him. As he opened the window we talked about our argument and he said he was sorry and offered to take me further in his car. He leaned across to open the passenger door to me. Immediately he opened the door I shot him. I had loaded the gun and had it in my hand when I came round the back of the car. This was about 4.30pm and it was daylight. I stood looking at him, then decided to take him to a hospital. I moved him into the passenger seat then drove up the road for a bit. By that time I had sort of gathered myself together and realised he was dead. It was no use taking him anywhere. I turned back and drove the back road to Aviemore, past Coylumbridge towards Loch Morlich. The car stuck in the snow down that way.'

He seemed to have put from his mind the penalty he now faced by admitting to the killing. In fact he seemed

The murder weapon

anxious to leave nothing out, engaging in what you might call a conscience-cleansing exercise, describing to me his shooting of Green as 'A mission of God.'

I spent a long time writing down everything he was saying and when he finally finished talking about Green and what he had done to him I asked him, 'Can you account for articles found in your room and at the garage which we have reason to believe are the property of a man named Hans Gimmi?' I asked him that, by then knowing perfectly well within myself, that Gimmi had suffered exactly the same fate as George Green. But the man sitting across from me had to tell me about it himself. So I was not totally surprised when he looked across from his chair and said, again without emotion 'I shot him! I'll show you where he is buried.'

VIII

So NOW I HAD A MAN ADMITTING TO NOT ONE, BUT to two murders. But I had to get some sleep. After many hours on my feet and travelling, I went to bed in a local hotel for a few hours. Next morning, armed with a warrant for Simpson's arrest from the Inverness Procurator Fiscal which had been flown south to me, I started out with Simpson and Sergeant Sloan back north. There was only one problem. I didn't know how long it was going to take because Simpson couldn't say exactly where he had buried Gimmi. He told me he could take me to the spot, somewhere in the Lockerbie-Dumfries area.

On that hot Sunday morning as we neared Netherfield Bridge, north of Kendal, Simpson pointed to the bridge and announced, 'That's where I threw away the .22 cartridges.' When I interviewed Simpson's friend, Arthur Sale, he told me the same story. So I ordered the driver to turn round and go back to Kendal where I arranged for the river to be searched when the tide was right. Weeks later I went back there and was present when a cardboard carton marked 'R.F. Rifle Club Mark II smokeless non-corrosive' was brought from the water. In it were ten smaller cartons similarly marked and each contained fifty rounds of .22 ammunition. Some days later police in Kendal rang me to say that a boy fishing just below the same bridge, had found a wooden box with even more ammunition. That was identified as having been stolen from Montrose Rifle Club on the night of March 6/7 ... just hours before Green was murdered. Simpson had been very busy that day! During my interview with Sale he admitted that he was with Simpson when the killer threw a .22 pistol and some more ammunition into the river Mersey. He told me the weapon was a single shot .22 with a fairly long barrel and no trigger guard. But for a long time the river was so high we could not find the weapon, although eventually it was recovered.

Around 1.50pm that afternoon, we met a Dumfries detective who accompanied us because Gimmi's body lay in that force's territory. As we drove up the A74, Simpson seemed almost as anxious as me to find the body. Again I cautioned him and warned him he need say nothing, but he then said he was doing this voluntarily. He guided us off the main road and on to a Forestry Commission road winding into Twiglees Forest. Handcuffed to me, he led us through a series of fire breaks to the far edge of one plantation where he said he and Gimmi had picnicked. Then, frustratingly for everyone, he said he was lost. But he went back, took his bearing again and then for a second time, he led us unerringly into the forest. Suddenly, some fifty yards in, he pointed at a spot on the forest floor and said, 'This is it.' The grave had been overgrown by moss and had blended into the ground. Had he not taken us there, it would have remained undiscovered forever.

I looked on as my colleagues gently cleared away the covering to reveal what could only be Gimmi's body. Simpson was calm, showing no sign of regret or remorse. He was simply doing a job helping us. Then, before heading up the A74, I arranged a photographic session at the scene and for a post-mortem to be held.

Again, despite being re-cautioned, Simpson insisted on pouring out details of his meeting with Gimmi and how he had finally murdered him.

Through the Missing Persons Bureau I knew that Gimmi, 24, was a textile designer working in Dunfermline but living in digs in Edinburgh. He had been expected at his sister's wedding, and the last his family had heard from him was a postcard saying he had left the Loch Duich area, in the Highlands, having been offered a lift to London via Edinburgh by a man who was a lecturer at Manchester University.

When their son failed to return for the wedding and didn't contact them, his parents reported him missing to Interpol who had then asked my own force to make inquiries at Highland hostels. It was this request that rang a mental bell reminding me that I had heard of Hans Gimmi before we ran across his name in Simpson's Manchester flat. Our inquiries for Interpol revealed that Gimmi, accompanied by a girl, had been at the Loch Laggan Inn on the Spean Bridge - Dalwhinnie road.

On that long journey north, Simpson told me, 'I met Gimmi at Inveralligin in Wester Ross. Hans had picked up a girl somewhere in the area and she was a Malaysian with an English-American accent. Apparently, she was on holiday. From there we went to Edinburgh, stopping for lunch at the Laggan Hotel, and I think we dropped the girl off in Crieff. In Edinburgh I stayed at a youth hostel and Hans stayed in his flat. He told me I could spend the night in the flat with him, but I didn't go because a woman went with him, a schoolteacher called Maureen. The next day Hans and I went to Loch Lomond, and that night I went to the hostel, but he camped out because he wanted to take photographs. The following day Hans wanted to go to Glasgow so I went with him. That night we stayed in Moffat and I slept in the car. He camped out. After that I went to Manchester, to Hathersage Road.'

It was clear to me that Simpson had deliberately avoided being seen with Gimmi because he was planning to murder him, and he didn't want anyone remembering they had seen him with the Swiss man. Although he went into great detail about the few days he spent with Gimmi, surprisingly, Simpson said nothing about the events leading up to the shooting. Police procedure prevented me from questioning him closely but then Simpson said that while they picnicked he and Gimmi had a difference of opinion over religion.

I knew then that the row had been Gimmi's death sentence. Simpson admitted 'I pulled out the pistol and shot him.' He had sent yet another of his 'converts' to God. Then, literally in the middle of nowhere, he stripped Gimmi of everything he owned... clothes, watch, camera and £30 in cash. Then he got the shovel from the car and, used it to bury his victim. When that was done, and it was perfect, no trace left, he went back to the car and drove down to Manchester.

Simpson went back to his life after the 'disposal' of Green. He told me that after shooting him he had driven around in the car for some time before changing the number plates and he only did so because he saw YUM 722 in a newspaper. He was to boast 'I went to London before I changed it. I drove down to Shepheard's Bush one day and back the next. After the details about the numberplate were in the paper I went down to London again, about a fortnight after it appeared in the papers. Sale and I drove about in the car quite a bit. He told me where to dump the number plates.'

I had called in at Glasgow on the way North and I left the Central police office there at 4.30am, with Simpson still handcuffed to me. That Monday afternoon he appeared in chambers at Inverness sheriff court charged with murdering both Green and Gimmi and stealing their personal effects and the car. A week later he was in court again, this time on petition by which time I had put further charges to him relating to housebreaking and theft in other parts of Scotland. He was remanded for trial to the High Court and, while in custody, was taken to Craig Dunain Hospital at Inverness for a psychiatric examination carried out by the medical superintendent, Dr Martin Whittet, and his senior assistant, Dr Ronald Caddell.

Police divers recover the missing registration plate

Meanwhile I was back in England, at Manchester and Derbyshire, where I was given marvellous help by two fellow clansmen, Chief Inspector Simon Fraser and his brother James, who had the same rank. Both were originally from Beauly, not far from my own birthplace. They helped me get the number plate YUM 772 from the Ladybower reservoir near Buxton, that same stretch of water made famous by the Dambusters Squadron who practised there before the raid in Germany. The charges against Simpson were what in legal terms, were called 'capital'. This meant that after trial, if a jury found him guilty, there was only one sentence the judge could pass. The death penalty. If he was sane, he would die on the gallows.

IX

ALMOST SIX MONTHS AFTER HE HAD SHOT GEORGE William Green and Hans Gimmi, the gnome was at last to stand in the High Court dock. But he never stood trial because psychiatrists told the judge, Lord Kilbrandon, that Iain Simpson was insane. He was, they said, and no one disagreed, mentally unfit. He stood there, a diminutive figure between two towering police escorts, seemingly harmless, as the judge declared: 'I hope this case will never be forgotten by those responsible for this country's mental health administration. If the system has given rise to serious public anxiety then I am not in the least surprised.'

Minutes earlier the crowded public gallery, every seat taken, had gasped in astonishment, when it was revealed that the man accused of two brutal murders had, only two years earlier, re-established his sanity by escaping from Hartwood Mental Hospital near Shotts, Lanarkshire. By successfully staying at liberty for twenty-eight days he had been entitled, under existing law, to reclaim his freedom. Had he been found and returned to the hospital, then Green and Gimmi would be alive today.

The Bogus Professor

For many years Iain Simpson had been destined for a life of crime. He was without doubt a danger from youth, a Walter Mitty character acting out a part in a make-believe life. He came from a race of men who, no matter what they do in life, will never fit in.

A small group of pedestrians and motorists had gathered around the crashed car. They quickly opened up a path when they identified a clerical collar and heard the wearer say, 'Please let me through. I'm a minister. I may be able to help.' Feeling guilty, unable to do anything themselves to assist the crash victims while waiting for the emergency services to arrive, they were relieved by the appearance of this figure of apparent authority. The man in black knelt down and whispered words of comfort to the seriously injured man and wife lying by the roadside. There was nothing that could be done for the little figures lying motionless in the back of the family's mangled saloon. The two children had been killed outright by the impact as the car skidded into a wall on the outskirts of Barlanark on the A8 between Glasgow and Edinburgh.

An ambulance and police came to take over. The bystanders started to drift away, shocked by the horror of the scene but impressed by the manner in which the man of the cloth had gone about administering words of comfort and assurance. When they looked back, he was gone. Back into the night from which he had appeared. No one had thought to ask him his name. He had obviously been a modest Samaritan who had responded to a cry for help, but preferred to shun publicity and the probing questions of the reporters who would soon appear on the scene. It was a reasonable supposition. But the man with the clerical collar had good reason for slipping away before the press arrived and for not wishing his photograph emblazoned across the front pages lest he be recognised for his true identity.

In a hall, a short distance from the accident, a small

'congregation' awaited the arrival of the popular pastor who had them to his regular Sunday night prayer meeting. This was the 'nice young man' who had come into their midst to do evening missionary work after his official congregational and pastoral duties were over for the day. The admiring handful who made up his Sunday night flock had no reason to suspect that their shepherd was far from what he claimed to be. Even were he to confess, they would have found it difficult to accept that the man who preached compassion and truth, and baptised their children, was not only a fake, but also a crank and a crook.

Their 'minister' had no right to the title 'reverend'. He had never studied for the ministry, apart from the time spent reading the religious books he had stolen from the churches and manses he frequently burgled. Nor had the self-styled preacher disclosed to them that he had been in prison or that he had twice been sent to a mental institution.

But there was an even more sinister side to the genial little Scot who each week exhorted them to obey God's command and carry out His will. In his own disturbed mind, he had convinced himself his 'ministry' had come about through Divine intervention and instruction. He had been commanded to 'change' people.... and a voice was telling him that if people resisted and challenged his interpretation of the word of God, he might one day be forced to kill them in order that they may receive instant salvation

Iain Simpson had been drawn to religion at an early age. By the time he was eight years old he had established a reputation with the local police as a petty thief.

Iain Simpson dressed in minister's clerical collar

But the police were quick to spot the then inexplicable connection between his behavioural extremes of religion and dishonesty. By his late 'teens his modus operandi was breaking into churches and manses. He once broke into a cemetery vault and smashed up the coffins. But most of what he stole from ecclesiastic premises he either gave away, threw away or returned to their owners. The only things he kept were books and tracts on religion. In his bedroom at home, he was building a secret library of stolen literature, all to do with the subject of theology.

Born in 1936, Simpson was brought up with five brothers and four sisters in a council house in Ramsay Place, Coatbridge, a few miles east of Glasgow. He left Kildonan Secondary School in Coatbridge aged 15 and became a grocer's delivery boy, then an apprentice draughtsman. Within a year he was back in school - this time an Approved School, on an order from the local Juvenile Court. He was sent there in the hope that he could be weaned from his persistent and unusual pattern of petty crime.

Hopes of reforming the unpredictable teenager were strengthened when he was thought ready to switch from the strict regime of life in an Approved School and answer his call-up to National Service. He was recruited as a private into the Royal Army Service Corps and eagerly accepted the discipline of army training, serving most of his two years in Germany where he picked up a reasonable grasp of the language.

By the time of his demob in 1959, Simpson had come to enjoy being the centre of attention while dressed in the kilt and he was no sooner back in Civvy Street when he purchased one. The kilt would open doors to circles of society otherwise firmly closed to a loner from a working class background and a history of petty crime. It was also the convincing sort of attire one might expect to be worn by a man who was about to project himself as the son of a famous Glasgow brain specialist.

X

NOW AS A KILTED CIVILIAN, SIMPSON RETURNED TO Weisbaden in West Germany where he had been stationed earlier. By this time he was also hinting at a distant relationship with royalty, a bluff he employed while assisting the son of a Dutch antique dealer to take some goods through customs. With his reasonable command of the German language, it was easy for the verbose young Scot to live his fake image and, having planted a belief that he had been a lecturer at Manchester University, he was occasionally invited to lecture to German students on a variety of subjects, including the complexities of the various religious systems in Britain.

His Dutch friend thought it strange, however, when an apparently affluent Scot asked for a loan to help him get back to Scotland. Simpson suggested there had been confusion over a bank transfer of funds and assured the Dutchman he would refund the sum (about £40) to the man's Amsterdam address within two weeks. Rather than send cash, however, the Dutchman said he would prefer if Simpson repaid him in kind by sending an equivalent value of antiques from Scotland. The glib-tongued Simpson assured him there would be no problem. He had relatives in Glasgow who dealt in object d'art.

But two months passed without even an explanatory note. Inquiries with the Dutch consul in Glasgow revealed that Iain Simpson had in fact been sent to jail - convicted of stealing from a church. The Dutchman wrote Simpson at his prison address and received a reply saying the outstanding sum would be settled if the Dutchman forwarded an invoice. The reply was signed 'Dr. Simpson', with the assurance that it had all been 'a terrible mistake'.

Simpson had time in prison to reflect on his future. He appreciated it would not do to pursue his previous double life, particularly in surroundings like Central Scotland or Weisbaden where he might be identified and exposed. If he was to continue with his 'divine mission' then he had to find pastures new. Where better, he thought, than the wide open spaces of the Highlands where there would be little chance of his bogus past catching up with him. It excited him to think that he would be able to move again among academics. Weren't those who sought the adventures of the great outdoors mostly university types - and among them students of divinity? 'After all', he convinced himself, 'I'm one of them too.'

For an accomplished thief, he knew it would not be difficult to acquire the gear to help him create a new image, under cover of which he could continue 'to do as God commanded him'. Once out of prison, Simpson moved south finding lodgings in Manchester, where a friendly landlady was pleased to have 'such a nice young educated man' as a lodger. He was no problem in the house, always paid the rent on time. Every now and then he took himself away for the weekend on a hitchhiking visit to the Highlands. When he left prison he travelled to Manchester, telling people he was a lecturer at the city's university. In reality he was washing dishes in the kitchen of the Queen's Hotel.

As he had anticipated, wearing the appropriate cloth-ing - anorak, woollen tammy, breeches and hiking boots and socks - Simpson found it easy to be accepted as one of the climbing and hill-walking fraternity. The others found the 'wee minister' a bit of a bore at times and he did seem to go on a bit about religion a great deal. Nevertheless, Simpson had no problem in youth hostels or boarding houses, finding sufficient ears willing to lis-ten and debate his outpourings on theology. To his delight, even in the remote Highlands, there was also no shortage of churches to break into or lonely cottages that might yield clothing or paraphernalia to further promote the image he portrayed. Besides, didn't he also need the means with which to finance his Walter Mitty existence?

But he found more than he bargained for when searching through the loft of an isolated cottage in Wester Ross. He pulled aside a bundle of rags and sucked in his breath in surprise. Before his eyes lay a pistol and a box of ammunition. A thought that had frequently exercised his mind in the past flashed again before him. If he was to fulfil his 'divine mission' the day could come when he might have to adopt more per-suasive tactics on a reluctant convert. He wrapped the pistol and ammunition in a spare shirt and tucked the bundle deep inside his knapsack. Now he had the per-fect method of converting sinners and, if not successful, the means of sending them to Heaven's Door.

XI

WHILE IN CUSTODY AWAITING HIS APPEARANCE before the High Court, Iain Simpson had been interviewed extensively by psychiatrists at Craig Dunain Hospital in Inverness. Dr Martin Whittet, consultant psychiatrist to Northern Regional Hospitals, told Lord Kilbrandon he was satisfied Simpson was insane and unfit to plead and he believed Simpson would have gone on killing had he not been caught. Asked to explain Simpson's attitude to murder Dr Whittet replied, 'Simpson felt he had really achieved something... he was doing this because the world was all wrong, according to his sense of values. He told me these people were not dead, they were merely 'changed'. He seemed to almost feel a sense of triumph.' Dr Whittet said that Simpson had given him the impression that it had been his 'divine mission' to kill. 'He said the two men did not measure up to his moral standards, so he decided he should kill them. He believed he was ordained by God to do it,' said the doctor.

While the medical evidence given to the court dealt with Simpson's fanaticism with religion, little emerged about his attempts at establishing a love life.

Back in Barlanark, his 'congregation' which had grown to around 200 within six months of him appearing in clerical collar and selling encyclopaedias, and where a real church was founded, his parishioners had begun to have doubts about him being a minister.... and about what was happening to money taken in collections. After being challenged at a 'congregational' meeting Simpson disappeared and the bills started to come

Simpson, his head covered, arriving at Inverness police station

in for overdue hall rental among other things. It also emerged that Simpson had approached several girls at his mission, asking them if they were courting. If not, he would ask them 'How about me? How would you like to be lady of the manse?'

In England, Simpson had charmed at least two girl-friends. Estelle, a hospital worker in Warrington, never had cause to fear him - except maybe when he joked that he could be the killer for whom the police in Scotland were looking. But by then the 19-year-old Lancashire lass was besotted and readily accepted his offer of marriage. Earlier, in a letter to her dated 22nd

February, he had written, 'Dear Estelle, It is a strange exhilarating pleasure to write in affectionate terms, about the glorious uplift in spirit (non alcoholic) that has dawned with our most happy meeting. However, perhaps I am being a bit presumptuous, you may have decided against our friendship, have you? I will at any rate proceed on the assumption that I have found the one who fulfils my ideal of womanhood, with high hopes that our feelings will someday have mutual aims. These words simply indicate a certain conviction of rightness, of truth, of beauty, that has come to me. It is as if the mind had suddenly 'clicked' and with the 'Click' I must end this very inadequate letter, Iain.'

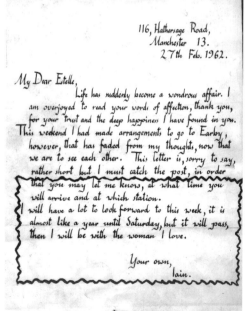

116, Hathersage Road,
Manchester 13.
27th Feb. 1962.

My Dear Estelle,
        Life has suddenly become a wondrous affair. I am overjoyed to read your words of affection, thank you, for your trust and the deep happiness I have found in you. This weekend I had made arrangements to go to Earby, however, that has faded from my thoughts, now that we are to see each other. This letter is, sorry to say, rather short but I must catch the post, in order that you may let me know, at what time you will arrive and at which station.
I will have a lot to look forward to this week, it is almost like a year until Saturday, but it will pass, then I will be with the woman I love.

                        Your own,
                                Iain.

One of Simpson's letters to girlfriend Estelle

74

But Estelle's dreams were shattered a few weeks later when detectives told her; 'Your boyfriend has been arrested for murder.' She later revealed, 'When I met Iain he told me he was a student from Glasgow University in Manchester to do extra studies. When we were out together, he talked about his family and I got the impression they were quite rich. 'I was always sorry when he had to go to Scotland without me. It was after one of his trips that he came back to Manchester with a car. I know now it belonged to Mr. Green. I noticed that when we were in the car he was always jumpy and he complained that the police had stopped him several times and asked him about the car. Then he changed the number plates and colour.' It was around that time Estelle light-heartedly asked Simpson if he was the killer the police were looking for. He laughed and told her 'I could be, dear.'

In any event it never entered Estelle's mind that her boyfriend could be capable of anything akin to murder. He did promise her that he would be taking her to Scotland to meet his parents. 'Some people tell me I was lucky not to have gone to Scotland with him, as he might have killed me. But I don't want to believe them. I want to remember him as the charming and kind boy I knew' she said.

Unknown to Estelle, however, Simpson had another girlfriend, Dorothy, who lived in Cheshire. At first swept away by the smooth-talking Scot, her interest in him had cooled. On the 26th March - having committed two murders within the previous three weeks - Simpson wrote to her, 'Dear Dorothy, You should be pleased to know that I will be unable to pay a visit this

116, Hathersage Road,
Manchester 13,
26th March,
1962.

Dear Dorothy,

You should be pleased to know that I will be unable to pay you a visit this week. However, that is to ignore the doughnut and magnify the hole. There must be moments when you will wonder why I insist that we remain friends, and tonight I will make an effort to express this thing I have encountered. For a long time I searched for what men call happiness, and in searching found pain, then we met, and I have found that happiness is a flower that surprises you, a song which you hear as you pass the hedge, rising suddenly and simply into the air and dying down again. This knowledge of happiness can only be described, as, the characteristic of immediacy that attends the awareness of value. I use the word "happiness" simply to indicate a certain conviction of rightness, of truth, or of beauty, that has come with your presence, a conviction which is beyond reason and which reason cannot, therefore, hope to convey. All that can be said is that I know that this is the right thing to do; that I know this is the right solution of the problem; that I know that this is the only possible way to end my unhappiness; and these things I know with a certainty that is both absolute and immediate. It is as if the mind had suddenly "clicked" and with that "click" I must bring to an end this very inadequate letter.

Iain.

week. However, that is to ignore the doughnut and magnify the hole. There must be moments when you will wonder why I insist that we remain friends, and tonight I will make an effort to express this thing I have encountered. For a long time I searched for what men call happiness, and in searching found pain, then we met, and I have found that happiness is a flower that surprises you, a song which you hear as you pass the hedge, rising suddenly and simply into the air and dying down again. This knowledge of happiness can only be described, as the characteristic of immediacy that attends the awareness of value. I use the word 'happiness' simply to indicate a certain conviction of rightness, of truth, or of beauty, that has come with your presence, a conviction which is beyond reason and which reason cannot, therefore hope to convey. All that can be said is that I know that this is the right thing to do; that I know this is the right solution of the problem; that I know that this is the only possible way to end my unhappiness; and these things I know with a certainty that is both absolute and immediate. It is as if the mind had suddenly 'clicked' and with that 'click' I must bring to an end this very inadequate letter, Iain'.

Having been told that Simpson had shot Green and Gimmi after becoming enraged that they would not share his fervour and passion for religion, and because he felt they did not measure up to his views of moral values, the shocked court also heard another Northern Regional medical expert, Dr Ronald Cadell reveal, 'Women were safe from Simpson, they were never really in danger as he would only interrogate men.'

Lord Kilbrandon studied written reports and listened closely to what the doctors had to say. In solemn tones his lordship recalled, 'The outstanding feature of this case is that the accused, in 1960, had been certified as a public danger and confined as such. He escaped from the confinement. He was not discharged as cured and when he was found again he was not re-confined, but was subjected to the old routine of a short prison sentence. I am not blaming anyone for this. It is the system.' Turning to the prisoner in the dock the judge declared, 'Iain Simpson, I order you to be detained at Her Majesty's pleasure in the State Hospital at Carstairs!'

Simpson was led away to spend the remainder of his life in confinement. He immediately adapted himself to his restricted surroundings and responded with commendable zeal and achievement to the treatment and therapy instructed by the doctors and nursing officers at Carstairs. He studied hard and proved brilliantly successful in an Open University course. By 1974 he had gained a Bachelor of Arts degree which was presented to him at a ceremony in Edinburgh and later he achieved an honours degree in science and social studies.

But I was not in court that day to see and hear the end of one of Scotland's most baffling murder cases, and certainly the most intriguing I had ever investigated. Instead I was in Inverness, in hospital, recovering from stomach surgery, a legacy of my mountaineering days! Maybe the struggle to find the Divine Killer had left its legacy?

XII

LESS THAN FOUR YEARS LATER I HANDED IN MY WARRANT card and, after thirty years service I retired. Over the years I had received many commendations, including one for my 'unstinting' efforts in solving the A9 murder. But instead of heading back to the croft Bunty and I had bought on the Black Isle, we took the children and travelled south westwards, to the shores of Loch Fyne in Argyll, where we were to run the Cairndow Inn, one of the oldest in Scotland, a spot where in 1875 Queen Victoria had rested travelling to see the Duke of Argyll at Inverary. And there we stayed until, for a second time, I retired, and this time it was back north to the croft at Munlochy.

But Cairndow was a big change from the police. We revelled in it and the children quickly settled down. It was hard work, but we had no complaints. And there was many a laugh. Like the time, and this all happened in two days, we had a couple named Shufflebottom booked in. Then another couple registered as Mr and Mrs Ball. Bunty asked where are you putting the Balls...? I couldn't resist it 'next to the Shufflebottoms, of course.' Then another couple booked in and it was like something out of a comedy act from yester-year. They were Mr and Mrs Cox. The page from that particular register has been carefully preserved!

Another arrival was a Mr Hillary, a motor cyclist touring Scotland. One day he was resting before lunch when our younger daughter Hilary came home from school, just having been told off by the teacher for not paying attention. She was furious and stormed upstairs, slamming the bathroom door. Bunty was just as mad. She shouted up the stairs 'Hilary, come down here at once and have your lunch or I'll come up and smack your bottom.' The door to room 3 rocketed open and Mr Hillary literally shot down the stairs and ran into the dining room. He was to tell the waitress 'I've never been called for lunch like that before!'

Ten years had passed since I had retired from the police and moved to Cairndow as plain Roddie Fraser. I first obtained the lease of the inn from the late John Noble of Ardkinglas having been recommended by Mr Noble's brother Michael, then Secretary of State for Scotland. Landlord John Noble was anxious to see the old coaching inn, on the Argyll side of the 'Arrochar Alps', function to its full potential. In earlier days the inn's visitors had included among others, Dorothy Wordsworth and John Keats. John Noble was extremely fair in his dealings with us and charged a rent of just five guineas a week for the first five years, an extremely reasonable figure even in the late 1960s. This fairness became even more evident later when Michael, by then Lord Glenkinglas, placed an extremely favourable valuation on the inn which enabled us to purchase the premises in 1978.

Looking to the family future, ownership inspired us to even greater efforts in an ongoing process of improvement to service and facilities. For more than a century, Cairndow Inn had been a focal point for the scattered community and a favourite refreshment or overnight resting place for weary travellers. In the days before motorised travel, it had been a staging post of the stagecoach service that plied between Glasgow and

Campbeltown. Under our management, the inn regained its popularity with the travelling public while losing none of its old world character and charm.

Life at Cairndow was maybe even more demanding on us than my years in the police. The hours were certainly long and the responsibilities on a licensee considerable. But there was great satisfaction to be derived from meeting new faces, making good friends and immense pleasure to be gained from doing our best to ensure that no-one went away unhappy after a visit to Cairndow. While still fit and active, we had looked to the family's future and had seen the move to Cairndow as a new challenge.

As families do, the children were growing up fast. They had adapted quickly to their new surroundings and been welcomed into the community. As each grew older, all four had learned to play their part in the day to day running of the inn, welcoming guests, helping in the kitchen, serving in the dining room, preparing the ten bedrooms or ensuring there was always a welcoming blaze in the fireplace in the lounge and in the bar. Oldest son, Douglas, was at hotel training college. In time he would marry and take over the running of the hotel, allowing us to move back to my native Black Isle where we would build for ourselves a house for retiral near Munlochy. Second son, Derry, followed in his father's footsteps and joined the police, but left after ten years to go into the hotel business. Marion had set her sights on a career in nursing. Hilary was in her early 'teens and still at school.

In the bringing up of our family, the running of the hotel and in the training of staff, we tried to set the kind of standards that had seen us successfully through our respective careers and also, by now, 20 years of happy marriage.

I am proud today to cherish two particular testimonials. One written by my former headmaster, extolled the personal qualities I displayed in youth and predicted a successful career for me. The other, from a chief constable, confirmed that I had achieved it. The first was dated 29th February 1936 hand-written and signed by Robert Strachan, MA, Public School, Avoch. It read, 'I am happy to be able to write in high terms of Mr Fraser whom I have known for several years. When a student in my Evening Continuation Classes, he proved himself to be intelligent and assiduous in his studies, courteous and considerate in his attitude to others, and punctual and regular in attendance. His cycling to these classes in all kinds of wintry weather from a distance of over five miles, showed him to be possessed not only of a sincere desire to improve upon his Day School education, but also of a fortitude of mind which was encouraging and an example to others. Of his moral character I cannot speak too highly, and I cordially and confidently recommend him.'

The other was the standard police retiral certificate which certified that Roderick Fraser had served in the Inverness-shire Constabulary from the 29th day of May 1936 to the 30th day of May 1966. On the final line which related to my conduct during my period of service, Chief Constable Andrew McClure had inserted in capital letters 'EXEMPLARY'. It was a final accolade of the kind which chief constables do not award lightly. Along with the one from headmaster Strachan, I gave it pride of place among the dozens of commendations and congratulations at my achievements during my 30 year police career – even the Certificate of Merit I was awarded from Acting Chief Constable James A MacIntyre on 23rd October 1962 'For your exemplary investigation into the brutal murder at Newtonmore of George William Green and for your co-ordination of inquiries excellently conducted by members of your own staff, members of Badenoch section of the Force and other Police Officers, culminating in the arrest of Iain Simpson who on 24th August 1962, at the High Court, Edinburgh, was ordered to be detained during Her Majesty's Pleasure for this murder and for the murder of another man, Hans Gimmi.'

XIII

HOTEL KEEPING STILL INVOLVED ME IN LONG hours and late nights. But between stocking and serving in the bar, looking after the petrol pumps, stoking the fires, helping in the kitchen and a host of other chores, I now at least had the minor luxury of being able to keep up with events in the outside world through the medium of the radio. As before, it might be the early hours of the morning before I could find time to read through the previous day's newspapers. But now the radio was on constantly in the hotel kitchen. And there was a portable transistor on a shelf in the bar which I could switch on and have an ear to the main news bulletins while serving a customer.

The A9 and Dumfries murders were far from my thoughts when, at Cairndow Inn, I switched on the radio on the night of November 30th 1976. The words of the announcer were sufficient to command my undivided attention for the next few minutes. The news stunned me more than a little and I lay back in my chair and remained in a reflective mood for the rest of the evening....

'A male nurse and a patient died from stab wounds inside the State Hospital at Carstairs earlier tonight and a local policeman died from his injuries outside the hospital when two inmates made a dramatic break for freedom. A second policeman is fighting for his life after being attacked with an axe.'

I listened intently as the announcer reported that armed police and tracker dogs were in the area and that a search and roadblocks had been mounted across a wide area. Quoting a spokesman from the Prison Department in Edinburgh, the announcer went on, 'a member of staff and a patient have died inside the hospital. We have had a head count and two patients are missing. They are Thomas McCulloch and Robert Mone. It is understood they are heading towards Biggar, and are armed with a knife. These men are dangerous and should not be approached on any account.'

The escape bid had begun in the recreation room at Carstairs around 7pm that evening. The nursing officer who died was James McLellan. He had been struck repeatedly with an axe. Outside the hospital local policeman, George Taylor, staggered to a nearby house bleeding from severe stomach wounds and a bad head injury, thought to have been caused by a blow from an axe. The killers hi-jacked his police van which was found abandoned soon after near Peebles. The body of the dead policeman was in the back of the van.

McCulloch and Mone were considered among the most violent and dangerous criminals held at Carstairs. It had been recommended by respective judges that because of the nature of their crimes they should both be detained for the rest of their natural lives. They are today still behind bars and will remain so until the day they die.

McCulloch, from Clydebank, was only 21 when he had been sent to Carstairs in July 1970, after admitting the attempted murder of the second chef and manageress of a local hotel. The court had heard that he had gone berserk with a revolver and a shotgun after a sandwich was served to him 'that was not to his liking'. After the row, McCulloch had gone home where he kept a private arsenal of guns of all types, bayonets and knives. He returned to the hotel brandishing the shotgun and a pistol and for 30 minutes held a party from the local Round Table at gunpoint, shot the chef, John Thomson, and the manageress, Lillias Rodger, and fired at Police Superintendents David Hutchin and Allan McKinlay.

Mone had been found insane and unfit to plead after subjecting teachers and children at a Dundee school to two hours of terror in November 1967. He shot dead Nanette Hanson as she shielded her pupils. Mrs Hanson was later posthumously awarded the Albert Medal, and a student nurse, Marion Young, also received the Albert medal for going into the classroom and persuading Mone to let the children go and hand over his gun.

The radio announcer reported on other events of the day before returning to the main story of the hunt for the psychopathic killers from Carstairs.... 'It was revealed a few minutes ago that a car containing the two men is being pursued by two police cars after being seen heading south on the A74 near Gretna and crossing the border into England. We have just heard that two men have been arrested by armed police on the M6 near Carlisle....

'We have also received a report that the patient who died in the escape incident was struck with an axe and knife and then stabbed with a garden fork while believed to be going to the assistance of the nursing officer who was killed. The Scottish Prisons Department has named the dead patient as Iain Simpson....'

XIV

MANY MONTHS AFTER IAIN SIMPSON DIED AND AS I ran Cairndow with Bunty, there came into my hands what, looking back, could only have been the final chapter in his twisted life. It was a Scottish Office report detailing what had happened that terrible night at Carstairs. It was to reveal to me for the first time just how violent a death the 'Divine Killer' had met, slower and more painful that the death sentence he both passed and carried out on George Green and Hans Gimmi.

He died in Carstairs, that lonely, forbidding fortress, standing on a high, barren site near Carnwath in South Lanarkshire. It houses the criminally insane, patients who are mentally handicapped and others who are mentally ill.

The Secretary of State for Scotland, Bruce Millan, appointed Robert Reid, Q.C., the Sheriff Principal of Glasgow and Strathkelvin to hold a public inquiry to determine just what happened on the night of Tuesday, November 30th, ironically St. Andrews Day, within and outwith the State Hospital. His remit was to investigate and report on the escape of patients Thomas McCulloch and Robert Mone. The inquiry started in the Memorial Hall at Lanark on March 21st 1977, and continued until April 15th. Most of the evidence was heard in public, but some, to safeguard the hospital's security, was heard in secret.

On April 12th the Sheriff Principal went to Barlinnie in Glasgow to interview the only two people in the world who knew exactly what had really happened that bloody November night in Carstairs.

Thomas McCulloch was born on March 7th 1950, and in his teens became addicted to alcohol and drugs. He had also sought professional advice to overcome his homosexual tendencies. He was committed to Carstairs on July 20th 1970, after admitting attempted murder of a chef and the manageress of a Clydesdale hotel near where he lived.

The court was told he had gone berserk with a revolver and shotgun after a sandwich 'not to his liking' had been served up. After the row, he went home where he kept a private arsenal of weapons; including the handgun and shotgun, plus knives and bayonets, and went back to the hotel. There, for thirty minutes, he held a party from the local Round Table at gunpoint before shooting the chef, manageress and two police Superintendents.

In the six years he was at Carstairs he settled down well, showing no signs of violent behaviour and, on the contrary, became increasingly co-operative. He appeared to mature and the conduct of the man, who was a time-served painter and decorator, was such that on June 1st 1976, he was granted the privilege of moving unescorted in daylight in the hospital grounds. But the hospital authorities told the inquiry that they always suspected he was too dangerous to be released.

Robert Francis Mone was born on June 25 1948; he had an unhappy childhood with a history of truancy. In his mid teens he was sent to an approved school and when his sentence ended he joined the army. In November 1967 he came home on leave from Germany determined to do something to get himself out of the army. He went into a school classroom in Dundee, armed with a gun, and held the teacher, Mrs. Nanette Hanson, and her pupils hostage for two hours, sexually assaulting some of the girls. A student nurse who knew him, Marion Young, went into the classroom to plead with him to put the gun down. He eventually did, but not before shooting and killing Mrs. Hanson. Both women were to be awarded the Albert Medal for their bravery, Mrs. Hanson's award being posthumous.

Charged with murder, he was found to be insane and unfit to plead and on June 23rd 1968, he too was committed to Carstairs under Section 63 of The Mental Health (Scotland) Act 1960. His assessment there was to read that he was above average intelligence and while a patient he obtained three 'A' levels and narrowly missed an Open University law degree. He took a keen interest in playwriting, but he was always argumentative, supercilious and his potential for aggression simmered just below the surface.

His medical officer at Carstairs was to say of him at the inquiry, 'He had a sadistic, schizoid, psychopathic personality.' Despite all these signs, he managed not only to become editor of the hospital magazine, but on October 7th 1976, just 54 days before the escape, he too became a 'trusty' allowed unescorted freedom within the hospital grounds.

He became friendly with McCulloch before that, in 1973, and although the authorities knew of this they felt there was no cause for apprehension. But, unknown to them, Mone and McCulloch had, towards the end of 1975, begun to think of escape and started to actively plot to get their freedom.

The Sheriff Principal was to hear in Barlinnie that the main plan to flee was born just two or three months before the actual breakout. Mone was to boast to the Sheriff Principal that he was the planner, but the Sheriff was to find that it was McCulloch's energy, ability to make weapons and escape equipment plus his skill in concealing them, that made the escape possible. 'McCulloch', said the report I was reading in the quiet of the night, 'accomplished so much so easily that they must have been tempted to think there was nothing in which they could not succeed.'

I read how Simpson was murdered along with Nursing Officer Neil MacLellan, the hospital's Recreation Officer, in a corridor near his office. The report was to say of the wee, almost insignificant man I had arrested so many years ago- 'He was a dangerous and intelligent man and at the time of his death was aged 40 years. He was a good workman and he taught himself to make and play a number of musical instruments.'

Despite the fact that Simpson had behaved himself, it was initially believed that he had been involved in the escape and had been murdered by his two accomplices, Mone and McCulloch. However evidence given voluntarily by them to the Sheriff cleared forever the idea that Simpson was involved. His only involvement came when he was caught, like his victims so long ago, in the wrong place at the wrong time. Mone and McCulloch both swore he had no part in their escape or the planning of it. The Sheriff was to learn that day in Barlinnie that, unknown to Mone, Simpson was destined to die the moment McCulloch set eyes on him in the social club.

As they prepared their escape the two men amassed an arsenal of killing weapons, a map, disguises, and false identification cards. They also had a flashlight and Mone had £25 hidden on his person. They had a rope ladder, three knives which were razor sharp, a home-made axe which was described at the inquiry as 'A frightening weapon' which could kill and was to prove that more than once, and a half-finished sword. Their original plan was to disable nurse MacLellan, but as McCulloch was to admit in Barlinnie, 'As I made the weapons, my desire to use them to kill anyone who stood in my way increased.' And at the actual escape he said he was 'possessed by an intention to kill.' The inquiry also were shown another two killing weapons, each deadly in its own right. Both were garrottes, one made with violin strings, the other with thick wire. They were not used in the escape but were found later when a comprehensive search of every part of Carstairs was carried out.

The escape was planned for a Tuesday night from the Social Club because it would be unoccupied at the time or, at the worst, only MacLellan and Simpson would be there. Once over the wall they would stop and steal a car and the escape would take place between 6-6.30 p.m. because the road outside was always busy at that time.

The murders were horrific, not only because of the injuries Neil MacLellan and Iain Simpson suffered, but because of the intensity and bloody frenzy of the attacks. When Mone and McCulloch burst into the office Mone threw Nitromors, a strong caustic paint stripper, into the nurse's face then started to struggle with him. McCulloch launched himself at Simpson and stabbed him in the head and as the two men fought for their lives the nurse bravely tried to escape from Mone to aid Simpson.

In the struggle Simpson somehow wrested McCulloch's knife from him and MacLellan, seeing this, ran from the office into the corridor, followed by McCulloch who caught him in the corridor. By now McCulloch had his home-made axe out and he attacked MacLellan with it. In the office, Simpson had got the better of Mone who was screaming for McCulloch to come and help him. Then Mone grabbed a garden fork, which should have been returned to its place outwith the office some time before and attacked Simpson with that until the smaller man collapsed. Mone then went into the corridor to help McCulloch, but Neil MacLellan, weakened by a serious throat injury after being stabbed by McCulloch's home-made knife, suddenly went down with McCulloch still punching and stabbing him. At 6.20 p.m. the bloodbath was over and both MacLellan and Simpson were lying, either unconscious or dying, on the floor.

The Sheriff was to say of Neil MacLellan – 'He acted with great courage and in the highest traditions of the nursing service. He could not have known McCulloch had a number of weapons and there is a nightmare quality in the way in which McCulloch was able to produce one weapon after another.' Mone cut the telephone wires to the outside world, then outside the social club as they prepared the last move of their freedom flight, McCulloch told his fellow killer to stay on lookout while he re-entered the building. And there, with savagery unsurpassed in most murders, he took his home-made axe and as MacLellan and Simpson lay there, perhaps near to death, he made sure they would never be able to tell what had happened by hacking them both about the head many times.

Once over the wall, Mone lay on the road and McCulloch used his flashlight to stop an on-coming car. He had a nurse's cap on his head and a false beard on his face. As the driver got out, the luck of the two manic killers was running out because as they tried to steal the car a passing police patrol van stopped. Inside were Constables Gillies and Taylor, who was almost instantly stabbed to death and his colleague seriously injured. The motorist managed to alert the gatehouse at Carstairs and the hunt was on. The chase was to last not one, two, but three hi-jacked vehicles before the two were caught on the M6, south of the Scots border by armed police from Carlisle. It was 9.14 p.m. when they were handcuffed. Just three hours and three murders since they put their escape plan on full steam ahead.

Mone and McCulloch are today still alive, still dangerous, but the public can rest easy. When they were sent down at the High Court the judge recommended that they were not insane, should not be returned to Carstairs, but because of the dreadful violence of their crimes they should both be detained for the rest of their natural lives.

Today they are still behind bars and they will remain so until the day they take their last breath.

When I laid that report down many hours into a new day at Cairndow, with only the gulls breaking the silence of another still dawn, it was with many thoughts of Iain Simpson, the little gnome of a man who had come into my life so unexpectedly, and who killed without conscience, but who must have fought like a tiger to stay alive, that terrible night in Carstairs. Had he lived, he would in all probability by now have been a free man.